With project sheets and much more!!

An illustrated book of

Critically Endangered Animals

Sally Taylor

www.artivive.com

ARTIVIVE

Hover your smart camera over the logo

C000243921

First published in Great Britain in 2020 by Sallyann Designs.

Text and illustrations copyright © Sally Taylor 2020

The right of Sally Taylor to be identified as author and illustrator of this work has been asserted by her in accordance with the Copyright, Design and Patents Act, 1988 (United Kingdom).

All rights reserved

No part of this publication may be reproduced, stored in a retrieval system, or transmitted, in any form, or by any means, electrical, mechanical, photocopying, recording or otherwise without the prior written permission of the publisher or a license permitting restricted copying. In the United Kingdom such licenses are issued by the Copyright Licensing Agency, Saffron House, Kirby Street, London EC1N 8TS.

A catalogue record for this book is available from the British Library.

ISBN 978-1-52726-682-7

Illustrated traditionally

Printed in Great Britain

An illustrated book of

Critically Endangered Animals

Sally Taylor

WWW.SALLYANNDESIGNS.CO.UK

ACCESS FURTHER INFORMATION

This book has further supporting information and activity sheets. Some of which can be viewed via the Artivivie app, others by visiting www.sallyanndesigns.co.uk/critically-endangered-animals-book-for-7-11-years/

You will need internet access or a wifi enabled mobile device to make use of the Artivive app.

Download the Artivive app from Google Play or Apple's iPlayer to your mobile device. On the pages where you see the Artivive logo, open the app and point the camera at the page, making sure the whole page is within the devices' screen. You will then be automatically taken to the relevant information for the page.

www.artivive.com

Alternatively, and for other information including links to helpful websites, you can visit www.sallyanndesigns.co.uk/critically-endangered-animals-book-for-7-11-years, where you can view and download extra material.

WWW.SALLYANNDESIGNS.CO.UK

ABOUT THE AUTHOR

Sally is an illustrator based in North Hertfordshire in the United Kingdom, graduating in 1979 with a BA (Hons) in Textile Design featuring animals on furnishing fabrics and toys.

After a career in graphics and environmental awareness, Sally revisited her illustrative skills, aligning them to her love of animals and in particular those animals on the critically endangered list.

A wife and mother with currently seven grandchildren who are her delight.

Special thanks to Jane Porter

AMUR LEOPARD

- Lives in S.E. Russia and N. China.

- Only 19-26 remain in the wild.

- Lives for 10 to 15 years.

- Lives in temperate, broad-leaf and mixed forests.

- Can run at speeds of up to 37 miles per hour.

- Under threat from logging, forest fires and industrial development.

ART|IVIVE

GORILLA

- Eastern Lowland Gorilla: 17,000 left. The eastern lowland gorilla lives in lowland tropical rain-forests in the eastern Democratic Republic of Congo.

- Western Lowland Gorilla: 100,000 left.

- Grow up to 4 to 5 ½ feet when standing on two feet.

- Cross River Gorilla: 300 left, scattered in at least 11 groups.

- Live in dense forest.

- In danger due to forest clearing, poaching & disease.

HAWKSBILL TURTLE

- Weighs 90-100lbs and up to 30 inches long.

- Lives in the Mesoamerican Reef, Coast East Africa Triangle.

- They feed on sponges, sea anemones and jellyfish.

- Endangered through capture on fishing hooks, Gillnets, egg collection, pollution and habitat loss. Also their shells are highly-valuable and commonly sold as "tortoiseshell" in markets.

ORANGUTANS

- Live high in the forest, rarely touching the ground.

- Carry their babies for up to 5 years.

- Live in South East Asia.

- Males have flanges and throat sacs.

- Shaggy reddish fur.

- They make nests in trees of vegetation to sleep at night and rest during the day.

- Live solitary existences, only occasionally interacting with a neighbour other than by calls.

RHINOCEROS

- 3 breeds of Rhinos;

  - Black: Lives in Nambia, E. Africa - 5,627 left,

  - Javan: 72 left,

  - Sumatran: 80 in the wild.

- Susceptible to natural disasters and disease.

- Subject to habitat loss, poaching and fragmented population.

SAOLA

- Discovered in 1992.

- Live in the Annamite mountains and forests of Vietnam and Laos.

- They have two parallel horns with sharp ends, which can reach 20 inches in length.

- Only seen on four occasions.

- Only 4,000 remain.

TIGER

- 2,400-2,800 Sumatran Tigers left, living in the Borneo and Sumatran forests.

- Affected by illegal wildlife trade, human wildlife conflict, habitat loss and fragmentation.

- Wild tiger numbers have dropped by more than 95% since the beginning of the 20th century.

- Tigers are mostly solitary, apart from associations between mother and offspring.

- Individual tigers have a large territory, and the size is determined mostly by the availability of prey.

ART IVIVE

VAQITA

- Live in the Northern Gulf of California.
- Caught and drowned in gillnets.
- Often found close to shore.
- Less than 20 living.
- Discovered in 1958.
- Grows up to 5 feet.
- Rarest marine animal.

ART|IVIVE

YANGTZE PORPOISE

- A smart, sneaky animal which is as intelligent as Gorillas, this porpoise lives in the Yangtze river in China.

- There are 1,000 left in the wild.

- Shy of humans, they stay below the surface. Locals called them River Pigs.

- These animals are in danger from fishing nets, propellers, and toxic waters from man's development activities.

SOME OF THE ISSUES

There are many reasons why there is such a large list of animals on the Critically Endangered list, the majority of these, if not all, are a result of how humans live on the planet. Many of the animals in danger live in underdeveloped areas, where the local people are very poor, or have huge resources that other countries wish to own. As custodians of this wonderful planet, it is our collective duty to care, help and support wherever and however we can.

Pollution

Many sea creatures mistakenly eat floating plastic, believing this to be food. The plastic stays in their guts, causing the fish or mammals to starve to death. Other pollution issues cause rivers to loose oxygen, become stagnant or worse, have harmful chemicals all which kill any living organism.

Deforestation, logging and ground clearance

In order to grow food to sell in international markets, countries are clearing large areas of forests, the homes of many animals such as gorillas, orangutans and the saola, resulting in their natural habitats declining. These animals can only live successfully in their own areas, many not able to uproot to find new homes. In some cases, like the Tapanula orangutan, they are all in danger of loosing their forest to flooding should a new dam be built to provide hydro-electricity for the region.

Illegal trade and fishing

There are many different types of illegal activities such as using gill-nets which catch all sorts of fish and mammals in the nets including porpoises and turtles which then drown. Other illegal trade includes catching and selling baby animals such as orangutans, killing large animals such as rhinos, tigers and leopards, for their horns, or skins; some just because people are able to kill them.

Climate change

The rate the earth is warming, causes ice to melt and therefore seas to rise. It also causes strange weather patterns such as rain storms or high temperatures which can cause widespread, uncontrollable forest fires, killing animals and humans too. The melting ice caps are cooling the seas which in turn moves sea creatures to new areas, where their food cannot be found.

HELP AND RESOURCES

Whilst putting this book together, I have come across some amazing charities who are mainly funded through donations and initiatives, some of which I have had the pleasure of supporting.

Ape Alliance
An international coalition of organisations and individuals, working for the conservation and welfare of apes. www.4apes.com

Explorers Against Extinction
Has a mission to promote the conservation of rare and endangered species and protect their environments. www.explorersagainstextinction.co.uk/about/our-story

Vecotourism
Uses interactive on-line tours to connect the general public with conservation projects and local communities in ecologically and culturally sensitive areas worldwide. We aim to nurture curiosity about the natural world, promote effective world citizenship, contribute to alternative livelihoods for communities living in areas of high conservation importance, and combat environmental degradation. www.vecotourism.org

Worldwide Fund for Nature
Works within four key areas; Putting nature first, Making food systems sustainable, Tackling the climate crisis and Thriving habitats and species, the Worldwide Fund for Nature is a global organisation. www.wwf.org.uk/what-we-do

ORANGUTANS – THE ORANGE APE.

Ian Redmond OBE
Ambassador, UNEP
Convention on Migratory
Species

Chairman, Ape Alliance
www.twitter.com/4apes

**Chairman, The Gorilla
Organization**
www.gorillas.org

**Ambassador and
consultant**
www.vEcotourism.org

The word 'orang' means 'person' in the language people speak in Malaysia and Indonesia, and the word for forest is 'hutan'. Thus, orangutan literally means person of the forest. It is just a coincidence that orang sounds very like the English word 'orange' which is the colour of an orangutan's hair, especially when back-lit by the sun as they clamber through the treetops.

Orangutans spend almost all their life in the trees, seldom coming down to the ground – they are the biggest arboreal animal in the world. They have longer arms and shorter legs than we do, and their big toe can grab against the other toes like a thumb, so they are much better at climbing trees than humans.

These differences between orangutans and humans are important but the similarities are even more interesting.

Orangutans are one of our closest relatives, along with the other great apes - gorillas, chimpanzees and bonobos. Despite them being our evolutionary cousins, they are all endangered species.

Why? Mainly because they are losing their forest habitat to agriculture, roads, mines and towns. Huge plantations have replaced natural forest to grow oil palms for vegetable oil and fast-growing trees to make paper. This is not only bad news for orangutans – it is bad news for us too.

The tropical forests in which they live play an important role in generating rain, storing carbon and keeping our climate stable. Orangutans play an important role in maintaining the health of those forests. They eat fruit and swallow seeds, which then fall to the forest floor in their droppings, miles from the parent tree. Orangutan dung makes good fertiliser, so seeds germinate well and grow into the trees of tomorrow. Ecologists call them the #GardenersoftheForest. This means that protecting orangutans is good for people who depend on the forest, and good for the planet.

We can all play a role in preventing deforestation by being careful to buy food, paper and wood products that are not linked to deforestation. And we can support organisations that help communities that live in and around orangutan habitat, such as the Orangutan Foundation www.orangutan.org.uk

NOTES

PATREON | Sally Taylor

9171814

The environment is so important; it how we use our world is critical. There are too many threatened places, and large numbers of wildlife species that are facing extinction.

Our best way forward is to help educate future generations - this book is a simple step.

Become a patron and share in the experience of creating and developing the journey with me.

As a Patron, you will have exclusive information about the art techniques and processes I use. Depending on the tier you decide on, you may have access to downloadable illustration too. Patrons help make things happen, providing the funds to print and publish a range of books to help educate children.

Join me for some fun art techniques, painting demonstration and tips too at www.patreon.com/user?u=13245395&fan_landing=true

"If we can teach people about wildlife, they will be touched. Share my wildlife with me. Because humans want to save things that they love."

— Steve Irwin

CPSIA information can be obtained at www.ICGtesting.com
Printed in the USA
BVIW121031220920
589359BV00010B/129